IMPOSSIBLE TO
KNOW

StoryPeople
Decorah

ISBN 978-1-937137-03-8
LCCN 2015915440

StoryPeople
P.O. Box 7
Decorah, IA 52101
USA

563.382.8060
866.564.4552 toll-free

storypeople@storypeople.com
www.storypeople.com

First Edition: *November 1, 2015*

To my beautiful Wendy Christine who chooses this us pretty early on each day & fills our life with laughter & delight & love. All of you. All of me. Saying yes.

To our dear friends Edna & Travis & Fiona & Evan. I hope you each know how much our conversations & passion & care are everywhere in this book. To my dear San Francisco EC & how that conversation about who we're becoming together is so very much at the heart of everything I experience these days…

& finally, to you, my dearest readers, who remind me with your stories that there is only one us, living full out, spinning endlessly into different shades of light. Thank you for the great honor & joy of being in this world with you all…

Other books by Brian Andreas available
from StoryPeople Press:

Mostly True
Still Mostly True
Going Somewhere Soon
Strange Dreams
Hearing Voices
Story People
Trusting Soul
Traveling Light
Some Kind of Ride
Peculiar Times (e-book)
Theories of Everything
Something Like Magic

IMPOSSIBLE TO KNOW

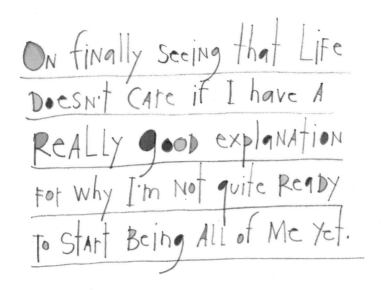

On finally seeing that Life
Doesn't Care if I have A
Really good explanation
For why I'm Not quite Ready
To Start Being All of Me Yet.

For a long time, I wondered if what you were supposed to do was be like all the other people you know, so I watched them & practiced in front of my bathroom mirror until I figured I had enough to start & then I tried being them. That didn't work so well, so I decided to try being me instead. That went all right for quite awhile until I figured out I wasn't being all of me, but only a few parts of me that had worked pretty well in the past. (Sigh.)

That meant there were parts of me (lots & lots & lots, it turns out) that got left out. Like the ones that didn't listen all that well because they were making up songs about spiders & sugary treats. Or the ones that said inappropriate things & laughed wildly & talked too fast & generally didn't care what anyone else thought. Those parts were sad because they knew (in some mysterious way) that as long as I didn't invite them to play, it would feel like I was doing someone else's version of life. Then it came to me: I'd rather be all by myself with a ratty beard & pants held up with an old blue rope than just be parts of me that fit in pretty well with how people expect me to be.

I have no real idea how everything happened after that, but it did & some parts were lovely & some parts were hard, but one day there it was exactly like I'd always imagined: a whole new life with a spectacular woman who didn't care if I did it right, but only wanted me to laugh & make up stories & watch clouds in the early morning without saying a word & not try to make sense of anything because she already knew most everything I think is completely misinformed by those parts of me that believe making sense actually matters.

So now, I love the world without apology & walk quietly with her by my side, without knowing anything about what I'll see, or feel, or taste, or touch & on those days when I'm convinced I might actually know something, I ignore it because it usually makes me miss all the other amazing stuff going on.

Also, we have a dog. Talk about impossible to know…

with all my love,

Brian Andreas
Decorah, Iowa
17 September 2015

trying my best to Make Sense of things that are ABSOLutely impossible to Know

& I think I figureD Out that if I stopped trying to do that, things would be Perfectly fine on their own.

Impossible to Know

It's important to know who you are. At least until you figure out that who you Are has Nothing to do with anything you think about tHat.

Those first moments are NeVeR where it begins. It takes time for us to come out from behind all the things we think we are.

but after that, if we're willing to stand there quietly, we start. To See & be SeeN. After that, we start to love.

Somehow, I got to thinking toDAY
is a good day to tell you all the tHings
I've learned so FAR iN my LiFe
(but without all the ENDLeSS DetAiLs
that'd Make your eyes roll back in
your head) & I figured I'd probably
Run out of SpAce, but at least I could
make a start of it & THeN it hit
me that I've really only learned one
thing: LiFe DoeS what it Wants
& it's a whole Lot more FUN if you
agree with WHAteveR it is.

that's All I've got so fAR.

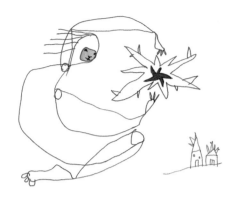

It is not that we hide from
the small, cold things at
the heart of us, but from
the Raging Heat of a
wild Self that Loves
this world without apology

& how do you live like that
without setting your
whole Life on fire?

Wild Fire

I'm finding the simplest way
to Happiness is to let myself
be happy with the things that
Make me happy

& also it helps to stop
Wondering if I could be
happier with other things
I don't know about yet.

Sometimes, it takes a lot for me to Remember to simply STOP & listen, because I get so busy giving my self directions that I forget I don't actually have all that clear an idea where I'm going.

I figured out today that I'm RiGHT about a Lot of things & I'm WROng about an equal Number of other things & the real problem is I'm never Sure which is which until a Long time later.

Early this morning, there was fog & as the Sun Rose around us, everything began to glow

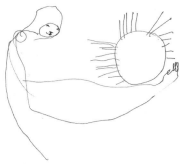

& it made me wonder what this world will become for us when we Remember in our Bones that even the Darkness is just another Shape of Light.

Even if you've tried not to Listen
your whole life, all it takes is
a Moment of Stillness &
you'll see how your heart has
Never Stopped inviting
you back to your Self

& do not be Surprised if you
decide to iGNORe this
a little bit Longer because
you'll think if your heART really
knew you, it wouldn't be this eAsy

Certain things
I've heard that
I didn't believe
the first time &
repetition doesn't
make it any better

Being who I am today
is always a lot easier than
being who I was yesterday
because, at this point, I don't
even remember it all that well.

I know there Are Things
about me you think should
Bother Me more than they
do. But they DON'T.

So. Could we just go on
with our lives & Could You
think about Something Else?

sitting exactly in the place
between where it's completely
still & where everything else
is falling Apart & Life
keeps Nudging me, whispering
Isn't it perfect?

& I'm trying to be polite,
but I'm Not Sure I see it yet.

I'm not sure where this is
going quite yet, but I'm
Pretty Sure I can
trust Life to go there
whether I agree or Not.

So comfortable in
her own skin
that she moves
like the wind itself

& when she passes
it's not unusual
to think to
yourself, It's time
to stop being afraid
of my life.

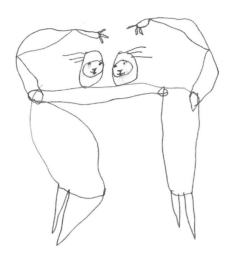

I used to think I was all
these different parts & then
one day, I discovered the
whole me & now I see
how much EASieR it would've
been if I hadn't fought so hard
(& so LoNg) to prove to myself
that the parts were somehow true.

Easy Decision

I've finally decided REALITY is pretty great just like it is, because when I used to think how much BETTER everything would be if I was Running things, I wasn't having A whole Lot of FUN.

BUS STOP
FOR
Mythical
Creatures

CASH
ONLY

Status Quo

ZOOM!!

Except for one or two exceptions,
I quite like people, as long
as I can get away
from them regularly enough
to remember that.

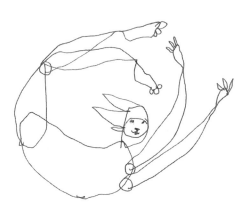

Sometimes I wonder HOW
MUCH TROUBLE I could've
avoided if I'd stayed away
from people who were almost
(but not quite) YOU, back when
I was almost (but not quite) me.

When I'm not sure what to do next in my life, I start with two things: First, I draw on napkins until my body remembers that my brain has no real idea what it's doing, so why are we even listening to it in the first place? Then I stop worrying about it because even if I just sat & drew on napkins all day long, that'd be a pretty good life.

But a lot of times I can only do this for a little while before I get HUNGRY & have to go make TOAST & then it's pretty clear what to do next in my life & voilá, problem solved.

I like to imagine impossible things, because when I only imagine possible things, I pretty much see stuff I already expect to see.

No matter how much
PERSpective
you've got on Life, it's
NEVER all that useful
to someone else. No matter
how much you think they
only Need to LiSten
Better to know that
you're probably Right.

Sometimes, I say stuff just to see if I believe it & OFTEN I don't, but Other people don't know that & they feel compelled to tell me where I went WRONG & it'd probably Be a GREAT CONVERSATION if I wasn't looking at the VEINS in their NECK thinking. All that TENSION can't be good for a person's health.

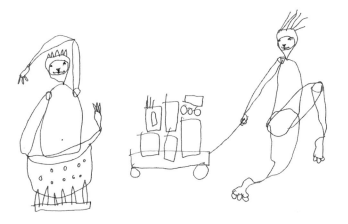

I had no idea that when I
invited Life to take over
that it actually would &
now I'm somewhere miles
away from any place I
know & Life keeps waving
its arms & grinning like a
crazy person saying
THIS. IS. So. great.

Crazy Life

this is an
interpretive
DANCe move
you can
only do
in your
head
(but still
you can
always tell
when someone's
doing it because
of the way they
smile)

Today, I'm in the exact place
in between two lives & you
may ask which I will choose,
unless you've been in the
in-between place before &
then you know to simply sit
quietly until your life chooses
you.

Sometimes I get busy doing stuff
I THINK is important & FORGet
the World does tricks I never
taught it, but when I NOTICE
I'll STOP for a Moment & clap
my hands & say Oh my, Where
did You learn to do that? & it
USUALLY jumps up & down laughing
& shows Me a bunch of other ones,
too & after awhile, I FORGet
what I thought was So Important
because WHat could be BETTER
than a Whole WORLD willing
to play with you any time you'd like.

There are times I still wonder
what I came here to do & then
I'll see you sitting there in the Light
& all of A Sudden, I remember
& it makes me laugh at HOW
OFTEN I forget such a Simple
thing AS LOve it ALL, no
matter what you do.

Simple Thing

Everyone I meet smiles
as if they already know
& perhaps they do, since
I gave up hiding my HEART
the moment we met.

Lately, I'm kind of torn between my OWN tRUE SelF & my idea of A new & iMProved Self that can Levitate & heal the sick (which Makes it eAsier for Me to just sit Around & watch tv & eAt chocolAte because I'M not sure I can tAke the pResSure of that kind of self.)

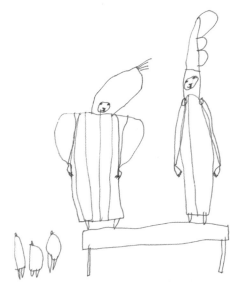

New & Improved

How do you explain this thing
where Love comes One DAY
& tAkes your life back &
SUDDENLY You can't reMember
what you found So iNteresting
About BeFore, becAuse you
are here & I aM here & have
You ever SeeN a WORLD
So BEAUtiful as this?

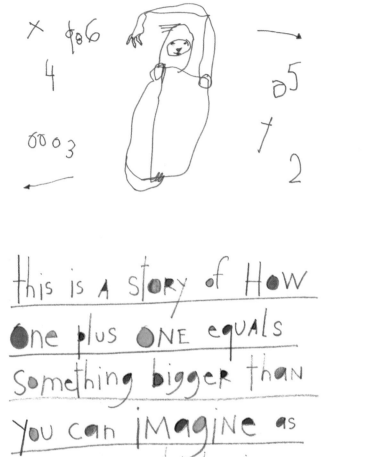

this is A STORY of HOW
ONE plus ONE equAls
Something bigger than
YOU can iMAgiNE as
long as you don't give up
TOO SOON because you didN'T
uNdeRstand the MATh.

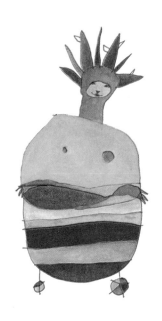

Each time I reach out & feel
your fingers twine with mine
Something in me settles
& I wonder how I ever
Believed I'd be fine
being Alone.

Someone asked me today
to be REAL & I said,
Do you want me to be Real
my way, or the way you
think real Should look?

& I guess that was a
bit too real for that
particular Conversation.

Actually
floating,
but it's hard
to tell
when you're
used to most
everything Falling

Being Real

I decided today I'm going to STOP explaining myself to people, mainly because I have NO Idea why I do half the stuff I do & the other half has such a SIMPLe explanation, like 'it sounded fun' that no one believes me anyway & they want to KNOW the real REASon, so I make up something that SOUNDS like it could be tRUe & I think to myself Well, maybe that ACTUALLY iS the reASon & I just get confused, so from NOW on the ONLy explanation I'm going to give is YEAH, can you believe it? & then I'll smile & shrug as if tHAt says it All & pretty soon, people will LEAVE me aLone.

the end.

Someone just told me that
if you can give up
all your expectations
your whole life would
change & I thought,
Well. Yeah, because
you'd be DEAD.

I hope to actually be as
enlightened as my principles
some day, but until then
it's pretty great to know
what enlightenment is
supposed to look like
without having to change a thing.

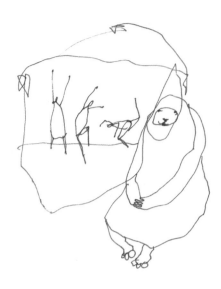

It's taken me a VeRY Long
time to appreciAte how much
ReaLity doesn't cAre what
I think about it & it just
goes on being its own fine
Self knowing that some
dAy I'll finally cAtch Up,
even if it's At the VeRy eNd.

In my dream, the angel said,
the way you want to be loved
might take a very different
life than the one you keep
holding onto.

& I thought to myself,
Why can't I just have a
dream with flying ponies
for once?

Today, I had a thousand things
to do until I remembered the
way you glow with love when
we touch & suddenly, it was
clear to me there is really
only one thing to do in this life
& always a thousand ways
each day to do it.

A Thousand Ways

Some people I know shake
their heads & say I'm Such
a ROMANTIC, as if that's
eNOugh to make me STOP
iN my tracks & SAy YES,
I see CLEARLY NOW that
feeliNg the GLOW of Magic
in everyone I hold dear is a
Complete Waste of time.

I had no idea when this started that there were so many people I'd love & often it feels like my body won't have enough skin to hold them all & yet each new day I wake & find I've somehow stretched farther & farther, so I don't miss a one.

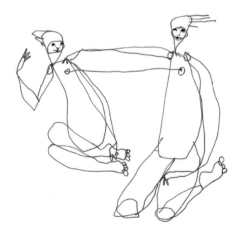

Regular Stretching

APPROPRIATE
WHOOSHing
Sounds!!

I used to put a lot more energy
into convincing people to
dance & laugh with me until
I figured out that Helping
people remember to do
things they should want to
do anyway is missing that
most of them already know
& they're fine with it for
perfectly good reasons.

I don't mind being busy
As long as it doesn't go
on & on & get in the way
of me spreading my ARMS
out wide & soaking the
whole World in.

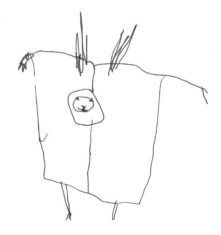

I promise the HEART of you
wants to DANCe & Sing &
Love WHOMeVeR you will
& it's as easy as Breathing
when you're FiNally reADy
& after, you may NOt eVeN
NOtice how quickly you forget
ALL the YEARS you spent
being afraid of exactly this.

The Heart of You

All the times I imagined
the FuTuRe, I never saw you
in it, so now when someone
asks me what I think will
Happen, even About the
Simplest things, I shake
my head & say. I don't know
for sure, but leave Room
for Something Wonderful.

On days when I wonder if the world is WORTH loving, I try to remember that finding MoRe reASons to Love is pretty much the MOst FUN THing you can possibly do!

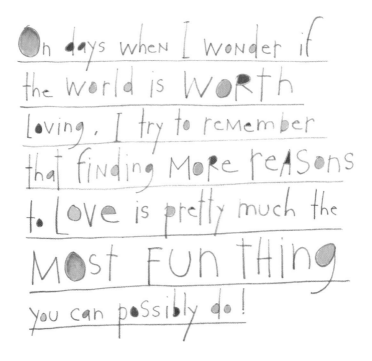

& also I stay away from people until that starts to kick in.

Today, decide to Pretend that ALL THE things that're wrong with the World are ACTUALLY Right, except you maybe can't see it yet & it's funny how that simple thing will calm you right down.

I was wondering today about what would be the PERFECT thing to do in my life because I usually have a list of ten or twelve things that might be perfect, but what if they're Not & then I noticed I was spending more time thinking about doing them than actually doing Anything, so I decided to just PICK ONe & if it isn't perfect, I'll stop & pick Another one & it seemed so simple that I looked AROund without thinking to see if it was a TRick, but it turns out it ISN'T.

This is one of those things
that make no sense until
about ten years after it
happeNS, but wheN you get
EMPtied it's because it's

ExactLy what you Need
before you FiLL UP
with everything YoU
imagine Life can be.

Fill Up

this is a little something
that says I Love You, but
there's no Pressure, so if
it's too soon, it's more like
a little something that says
Hey, I like your Shoes.

At first glance, they might
not seem to go together

until you see how they
glow a little every
time they touch.

Sometimes, when people ask about you, I WONDER what I should tell them

& often, while I'm standing there wondering, they simply smile & reach out & touch me, as if to Remind me that you are My Heart, as if I could somehow have missed that.

Reminder

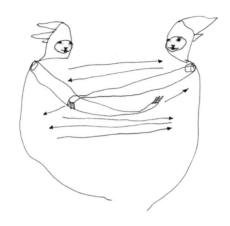

It is simple really.
I will always be
glad you took my
hand that very first
day & said yes.

First Day

It's not that I can't live
without you. It's that
I live so much with you
that I don't want to miss
A bit of it.

Real Choice

I hope you know by Now
that even when you are
far away, I will wait there
beside you. my skin against
your skin, until you find
your way Home.

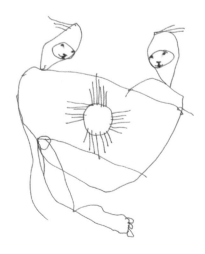

Coming Home

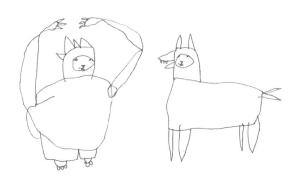

there is a thing in Me that
raises its head & scents the AiR
until it knows exactly where
you are as you Move through
the dAy & it is the thing that
pays no attention to words
About Love & only to the
feel of you by my Side.

All I can tell you is there is a moment
where you finally STOP & refuse
to pretend this life is not yours
& suddenly being STRONG looks
a lot like Laughing & Crying &
Dancing & Listening Deeply
to the people you love

& now & then, you'll look back
at that old way & wonder
how you ever believed that
Life was Something to endure.

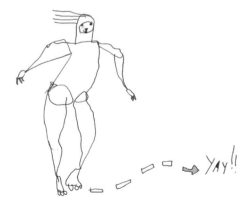

YAY!!

I find I think about you MOST when I'm far away, because when I'm Right there with you, We're too Busy to think.

There are people who believe
we stand ALONE, whole &
complete
& perhaps that's TRUE,
            but all I know is there
are parts of Me that would
not be if they had NOT
COME ALive with you.

this May look empty,
but that's exactly
what it takes
before it can hold
everything you
imagine Life
to be

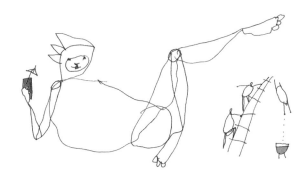

Today is one of those days when
no matter how MUCH there is
to do, I still feel the WORLD
purring all around me & it makes
me smile & wonder if it
ever looks at us & shakes its
head & thinks. These people are NUTS.

I know I've said I have No words for how I feel about YOU, but Actually it's more like I have lots & lots of WORDS & they all jump up & down at oNCe & it gets so exciting in there that I forget to tAlk.

Forget to Talk

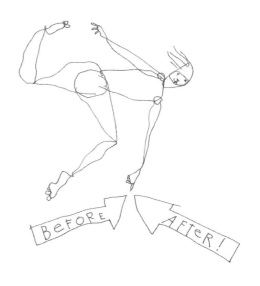

It only took a moment
to decide to love you
wildly with my whole
Heart & the thing that
Amazes me again
& again is that it really
is as Simple as that.

Quick Decision

Walking away from all the things
I know because something in me
whispers. It's time to not know
again

 & this time I think I might
be Ready to hear the secrets
the world has kept safe for
me my whole life.

Ready to Hear

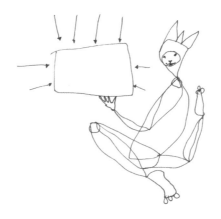

These are words that say
exActly what you need
to hear in this moment, as Long
As you're willing to close
your eyes & Listen deeply
& ignore EVERYTHING
you think you know up till NOW.

Exactly Now

Maybe this is how it always is, that we think we go into the world alone & lose ourselves there until, at last, Love calls our name & suddenly we Remember the way home.

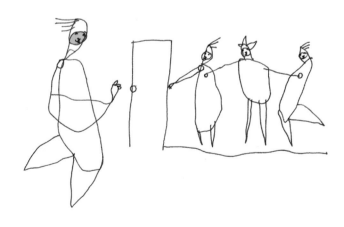

Remember Home

There are things that only
you can do & you'll know it
when you stumble on them
& it feels like flying &
usually it happens about
the time you quit trying
to do everything right.

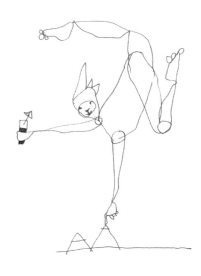

Right Timing

That thing you want to do
with your WHOLe HeArt?
Yeah. Go do it.

That thing you KINDa
want to do if it EVER
WORKS out?
Let it go. FREE your
MiNd for something gREAt.

I hope someday you see
this is all Life wants:
for you to be your own
kind of beautiful & not
the kind that makes you
forget who you are.

Life Wants

One of those perfect Days
when I feel like I'm Ready
to Open Wide & invite in
the whole World

as long As you're all
clear I don't Mean
everyone At once.

Trust is a Lot easier
when you quit WORRYING
about what could go wrong
& remember how much Life
you're going to Live, no
matter what happens.

The two things I know

No. 1: If you have a choice, pick a big ADVENTURE, because Life will give you exactly that & exactly the people who're Big enough to love the world right along with you

& No. 2: You always have a choice.

A note from Brian

Sometimes it seems to me that the way I experience the world is as one sprawling conversation. Sometimes it's in words, but just as often, it's not. Cooking together is what first comes to mind. The way we sit around the kitchen table & share the taste of things that, for the longest time, were only possibilities waiting quietly in the piled stacks of cookbooks. How that leads easily into ripples of laughter & deep gratitude for the adventure of this life. After that, the conversation that requires no words: the intertwined fingers of warm hands, or bodies woven together, filled with tenderness & heat.

But always I find myself coming back to words. Because I love their deliciousness, how they spark like lightning between us, crackling with the joy & exuberance of being alive. So, it's funny to me that while I think I'll always revel in words & the ways they create worlds, a few weeks ago, I decided to stop using them to explain things. I just stopped. No more explaining, either to myself or other people.

Because, right now, it feels like it's enough to play with them, letting them make happy noises when they're in the mood & letting them stretch & sleep by the fire when they're not. (See? You can already tell how having a dog is changing everything...)

Here's what I'm finding: that if you don't explain a whole lot, people & things get to be exactly what they are. Suddenly, there are connections everywhere & there's no real separation between you & the world. You start to understand in your bones that always wanting an explanation is a form of blindness. That your need to know is in the way of simply being here with the lovely wildness of it all.

& as you'd suspect, that's changing my work all over again. As I get more curious about not knowing anything, I find I'm playing only with things that want to play back. Suddenly, it's easy to stop trying to make everything go my way. My greatest joy is to simply delight in the all of it. I hope you feel that bubbling up, too, in this, my thirteenth book.

& just so you know, while I've got new stories popping up regularly over at **storypeople.com**, if you want to check out some of the other work I do, drop in to **brianandreas.com**. Or follow me on Instagram: **@brianandreas**. But fair warning, you should probably set aside plenty of time, because there's some serious play going on there...